PROFESSIONAL SINGER'S POP/ROCK FAKE BOOK

WOMEN'S EDITION

635

781.66
e.1

This publication is not for sale in
the EU and/or Australia
or New Zealand.

ISBN 0-7935-5989-8

HAL•LEONARD®
CORPORATION

7777 W. BLUEMOUND RD. P.O. BOX 13819 MILWAUKEE, WI 53213

Visit Hal Leonard Online at
www.halleonard.com

CONTENTS

ALL I NEED IS A MIRACLE

Words and Music by CHRISTOPHER NEIL
and MICHAEL RUTHERFORD

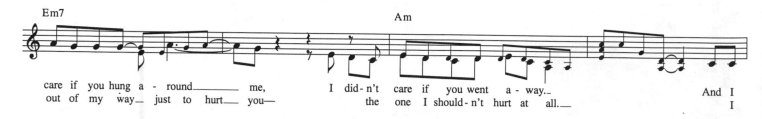

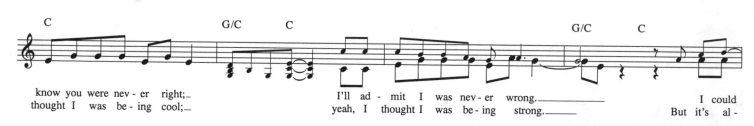

ANGEL OF THE MORNING

Words and Music by
CHIP TAYLOR

me _____ through the tears ____ of the day, ___

(me) _____

____ of the years, ____ ba - by, ba - by.

Just call me an - gel of the morn - ing, __ an - gel. Just touch my cheek be - fore__ you leave me, ba - by.

Play 3 times

Just call me an - gel of the morn - ing, an - gel. Then slow - ly turn a - way from me.

BABY, WHAT YOU WANT ME TO DO

Words and Music by
JIMMY REED

1. You got me run - nin', you got me hid - in', you got me
up, go - in' down, go - in'
peep - in', got me hid - in', got me

run, hide, hide, run, an — y way you wan - na let it roll. __ Yeah, yeah,
up, down, down, up, an — y way you wan - na let it roll. __
peep, hide, hide, peep, an — y way you wan - na let it roll.

yeah. __ You got me do - in' what you want me, ba - by, why you wan - na let

1, 2 Repeat ad lib.; instrumental verses may be added | **Last time**

go?
2. Go - in'
3. Got me
go?

BEAUTIFUL IN MY EYES

Words and Music by
JOSHUA KADISON

BLACKBIRD

Words and Music by JOHN LENNON
and PAUL McCARTNEY

BLUE SUEDE SHOES

Words and Music by
CARL LEE PERKINS

*Melody is written an octave higher than sung.

BUILD ME UP, BUTTERCUP

Words and Music by TONY McCAULEY
and MICHAEL D'ABO

Bubble Gum Shuffle

N.C.

Why do you

C   E7   E7#5   F

build me up, (build me up) but-ter-cup ba-by, just to let me down (let me down) and

F/G   C/G   G   C   E7   E7#5

mess me a-round? And then worst of all (worst of all) you nev-er call, ba-by, when you

F   F/G   C/G   G   C

say you will, (say you will) but I love you still. I need you (I need you) more than an-

C/Bb   F/A   Fm/Ab

-y-one, dar-ling. You know that I have from the start. So

Fine last time

C   G7   F   C   Dm7   C

build me up, (build me up) but-ter-cup, don't break my heart.

N.C.   C   G   Bb   F

("I'll be o-ver at ten," you tell me time and a-gain, but you're late.
To you I'm a toy, but I could be the boy* you a-dore,

C   Dm   Dm9   G7   C   G

I wait a-round, and then I run to the door, I can't take
if you just let me know. And though you're un-true, I'm at-tract-

Bb   F   C   Dm   Em   F6

an-y-more, it's not you, you let me down a-gain.
-ed to you all the more. Why do I need you so? (Hey, hey, hey!)

Dm   C/G   Dm/F   Em

Ba-by, ba-by, try to find (Hey, hey, hey!) a lit-tle time and

A7   Dm   D7

I'll make you hap-py, I'll be home, I'll be be-side the phone, wait-ing for

G   F/G   G   F/G   G   F/G

2nd time D.S. al Fine

you. Ooh. Ooh. Why do you

*Women singers could sing "girl" instead of "boy."

BUT IT'S ALRIGHT

Words and Music by JEROME L. JACKSON
and PIERRE TUBBS

Moderately, with a groove

Play 4 times

(Bass enters 2nd time)

(groove continues)

You don't know   how   I   feel..   You'll
one   day   you'll   see   you'll
There's one thing   I   wan-na say,   you'll

nev-er know   how   I   feel.   When I   need-ed you   to
nev-er find   a   guy   like me   who'll love you   right   both
meet a   guy*   who'll make   you pay,   who will treat you bad   and

come a-round,   you'd al-ways try   to   put me down..   Well, I
day and night.   You'll nev-er have to wor-ry   'cause it's al-right.   Oh, but
make you sad.   And you will ru-in   the love you had.   Oh, but

know,   girl,*   be-lieve me when I   say   that you   are
I'm tell-in' you, girl,*   and I   know that it's true   I   was
I hate   to   say I told you so,   ba-by,   you

To Coda ⊕

sure-ly, sure-ly gon-na pay.
n't made to love on-ly you.   Girl,*   but it's al-right,   al-right, girl.*   You keep
got to reap what you sew.

1   **2**

hurt-in' me,   but it's al-right.   Hey, now it's al-right,   oh, yeah.

*Women singers could sing "yeah" instead of "girl"; "girl" instead of "guy".

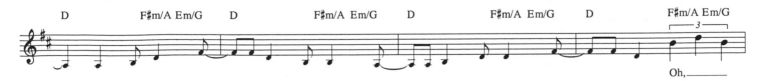

(groove continues)

Oh,_____

oh, yeah,__ my, my, my ba - by,_____ I said__

D.S. al Coda

it's al - right,__ al - right girl.*_ Hey, now it's al - right, al - right, girl.*_

CODA

right, girl.*__ You are pay - in' now,_____ but it's al - right.

Repeat ad lib. | **Last time**

Good - bye, love, good - bye, girl.*__ You're it's al - right.

Can You Feel The Love Tonight
from Walt Disney Pictures' THE LION KING

Music by ELTON JOHN
Lyrics by TIM RICE

CAN'T HELP FALLING IN LOVE

Words and Music by GEORGE DAVID WEISS,
HUGO PERETTI and LUIGI CREATORE

THE CLOSER I GET TO YOU

Words and Music by JAMES MTUME
and REGGIE LUCAS

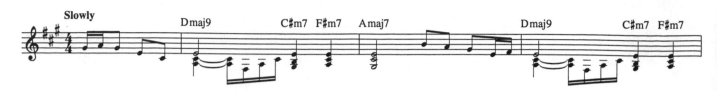

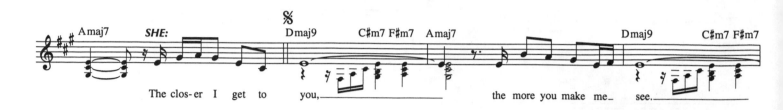

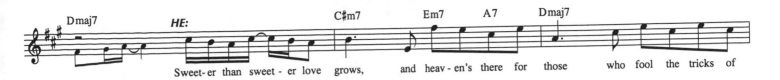

Sweet- er than sweet - er love grows, and heav- en's there for those who fool the tricks of

time.____ With the hearts of love, they find true love____ in a spe- cial way.____ The clos- er I get to

CODA

The clos - er I get to you,____ the more you make me____ see.____

By giv - ing you all I've got,____ your love has cap - tured me.

(They Long to Be)
CLOSE TO YOU

Lyric by HAL DAVID
Music by BURT BACHARACH

We present a useful solo edition of the song, rather than The Carpenter's specialty arrangement.
*Women singers could sing "girls" instead of "boys."

COME MONDAY

Words and Music by
JIMMY BUFFETT

COPACABANA
(At the Copa)

Words by BRUCE SUSSMAN and JACK FELDMAN
Music by BARRY MANILOW

CRYING

Words and Music by ROY ORBISON
and JOE MELSON

DAYDREAM BELIEVER

Words and Music by
JOHN STEWART

Moderately

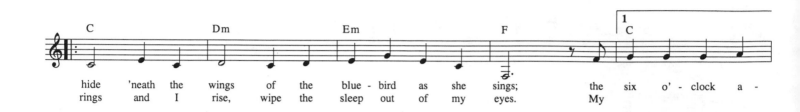

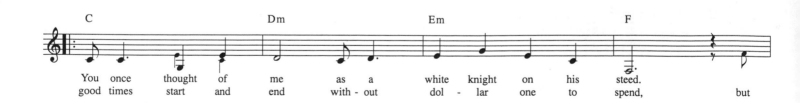

C | Am | D7 | G7

Now you know___ how hap - py I can be._____ Oh, and our

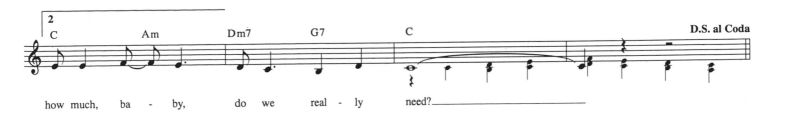

2

C | Am | Dm7 | G7 | C

D.S. al Coda

how much, ba - by, do we real - ly need?_____

CODA

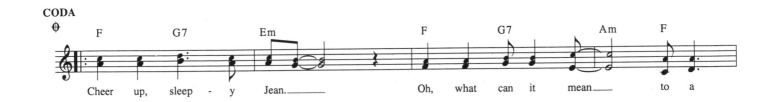

F | G7 | Em | F | G7 | Am | F

Cheer up, sleep - y Jean._____ Oh, what can it mean___ to a

Repeat ad lib.

C | F | C | Am | D7 | G7

day - dream be - liev - er and___ a Home - com - ing Queen?_____

C | G7sus | C | G7sus | C

(Instrumental)

DIFFERENT DRUM

Words and Music by
MICHAEL NESMITH

DON'T LET ME BE LONELY TONIGHT

Words and Music by
JAMES TAYLOR

DREAM BABY
(How Long Must I Dream)

Words and Music by
CINDY WALKER

Moderately

Dream ba-by got____ me dream-in' sweet dreams the whole day through,

dream ba-by got____ me dream-in' sweet dreams night time, too.

I love you and____ I'm dream-in' of you. That won't do.____

Dream ba-by, make____ me stop my dream-in'. You can make my dreams come true.

Sweet dream ba-by, sweet dream

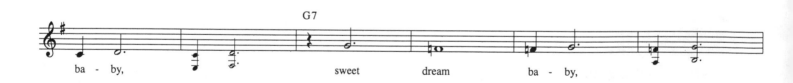

ba-by, sweet dream ba-by,

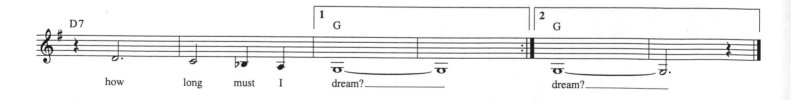

how long must I dream?____ dream?____

1. G
2. G

DREAM LOVER

Words and Music by
BOBBY DARIN

* "Girl" may be changed to "boy" throughout, plus similar adaptations.

DUST IN THE WIND

Words and Music by
KERRY LIVGREN

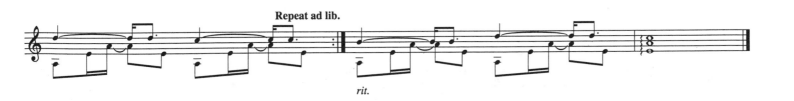

ENDLESS LOVE

Words and Music by
LIONEL RICHIE

EVERY BREATH YOU TAKE

Written and Composed by
STING

*Melody line is notated an octave higher than sung.

EVERY HEARTBEAT

Words and Music by AMY GRANT,
WAYNE KIRKPATRICK and CHARLIE PEACOCK

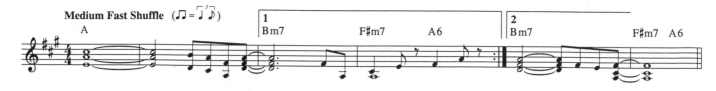

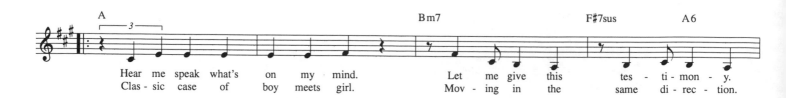

Hear me speak what's on my mind.
Clas - sic case of boy meets girl.

Let me give this tes - ti - mo - ny.
Mov - ing in the same di - rec - tion.

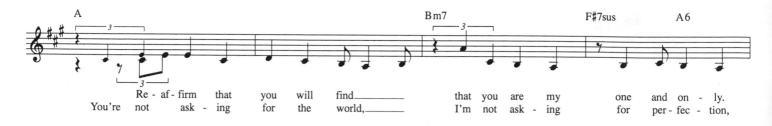

Re - af - firm that you will find____ that you are my one and on - ly.
You're not ask - ing for the world,____ I'm not ask - ing for per - fec - tion,

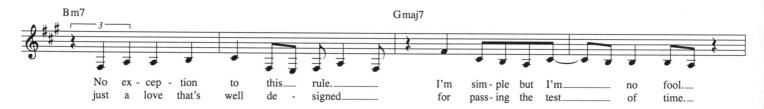

No ex - cep - tion to this____ rule.____ I'm sim - ple but I'm____ no fool.
just a love that's well de - signed____ for pass - ing the test____ of time.__

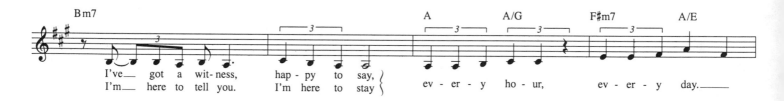

I've__ got a wit - ness, hap - py to say,
I'm__ here to tell you. I'm here to stay

ev - er - y ho - ur, ev - er - y day.__

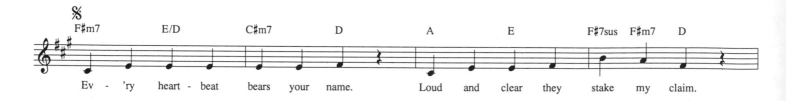

Ev - 'ry heart - beat bears your name. Loud and clear they stake my claim.

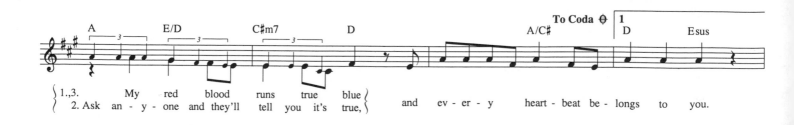

1.,3. My red blood runs true blue
2. Ask an - y - one and they'll tell you it's true,

and ev - er - y heart - beat be - longs to you.

longs to you.

CODA

longs to you._____ Woo._____ Ooh. Ah._____

Yeah, sure, may - be I'm on the edge,_ but I love you, ba - by, and like I said,

Original feel

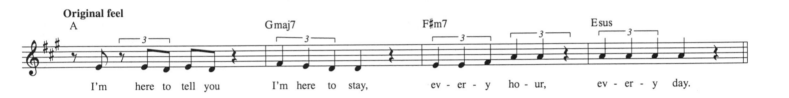

I'm here to tell you I'm here to stay, ev - er - y ho - ur, ev - er - y day.

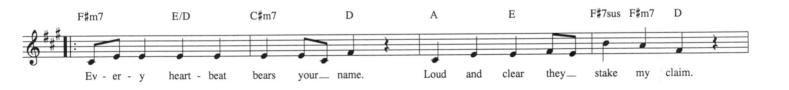

Ev - er - y heart - beat bears your_ name. Loud and clear they_ stake my claim.

Ask an - y - one and they'll tell you it's true that Ev - er - y_ heart - beat be - longs to you.
My red blood runs true blue.

EVERYTHING I OWN

Words and Music by
DAVID GATES

Moderate

You shel-tered me___ from harm,

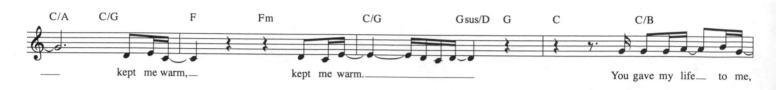

kept me warm,___ kept me warm._____ You gave my life___ to me,

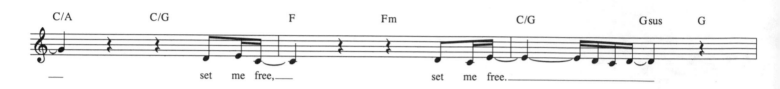

set me free,___ set me free._____

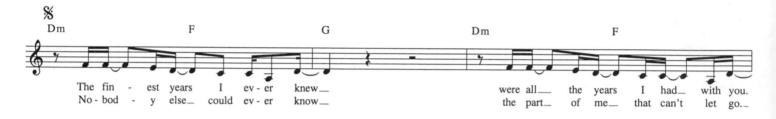

The fin-est years I ev-er knew___ were all___ the years I had___ with you.
No-bod-y else___ could ev-er know___ the part___ of me___ that can't let go.___

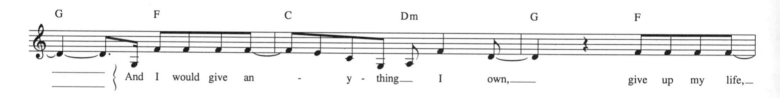

And I would give an - y-thing___ I own,___ give up my life,___

my heart,___ my home.___ I would give ev - 'ry-thing___ I own___

To Coda

just to have___ you back a-gain.___ You taught me___ how to love,

what it's of,___ what it's of._____ You nev-er said___ too much but

still you showed the way,— and I knew— from watch - ing you.—

CODA

Is there some - one you know,— you're lov - ing them so,— but

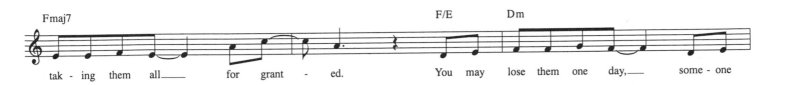

tak - ing them all— for grant - ed. You may lose them one day,— some - one

takes them a - way— and they don't— hear the words you long— to say.— I would give an -

- y - thing— I own,— give up my life,— my heart,— my home..

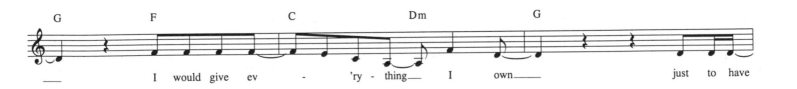

— I would give ev - 'ry - thing— I own— just to have

— you back a - gain,— just to touch— you once a - gain.—

EVERYTIME YOU GO AWAY

Words and Music by
DARYL HALL

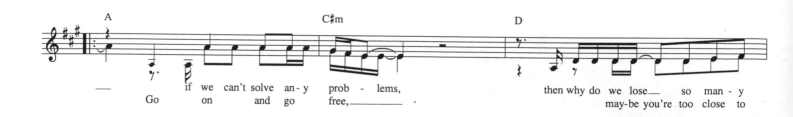

me with_ you. Ev - 'ry - time you go a - way,___ you take a piece of

me with_ you.

I can't_ go on_____ sing - ing the same_ theme,_ 'cause ba - by, can't_ you see we got

ev - 'ry - thing go - ing on and on_ and on._____ Ev - 'ry - time you go a - way,___

you take a piece of me with_ you. Ev - 'ry - time you go.

EVERLASTING LOVE

Words and Music by BUZZ CASON
and MAC GAYDEN

THE FIRST TIME EVER I SAW YOUR FACE

Words and Music by
EWAN MacCOLL

FIELDS OF GOLD

Written and Composed by
STING

FIRE AND RAIN

Words and Music by
JAMES TAYLOR

*Women singers might omit this word.

GET BACK

Words and Music by JOHN LENNON
and PAUL McCARTNEY

Jo Jo was a man who thought he was a lon-er, but he knew it could-n't last. Jo
Instrumental

Sweet Lor-et-ta Mar-tin thought she was a wom-an, but she was an-oth-er man. All
Instrumental

Jo left his home in Tuc-son Ar-i-zo-na, for some Cal-i-for-nia grass. Get back!

the girls a-round her say she's got it com-ing, but she gets it while she can. Get back!

Get back! Get back to where you once be-longed. Get back!

Get back! Get back to where you once be-longed.

Spoken: Get back, Jo Jo.

Spoken ad lib:

Get back, Loretta, your momma's waitin' for you
Wearin' her high heel shoes and a low neck sweater.
Get back home, Loretta.

GOOD LOVIN'

Words and Music by RUDY CLARK
and ARTHUR RESNICK

GOT MY MIND SET ON YOU

Words and Music by
RUDY CLARK

GET UP STAND UP

Words and Music by BOB MARLEY
and PETER TOSH

GREAT BALLS OF FIRE

Words and Music by OTIS BLACKWELL
and JACK HAMMER

HAPPY TOGETHER

Words and Music by GARRY BONNER
and ALAN GORDON

Steady, solid beat

I-mag-ine

me and you,___ I do.   I think a-bout you day and night.___ It's on-ly right   to think a-bout the

one you love,___ and hold him tight,   so hap-py to-geth-er._____   If I should

(Background)
Call   you   up,   ease   my   mind,

call you up,___ in-vest a dime,   and you say you be-long to me___ and ease my mind, i-mag-ine how the

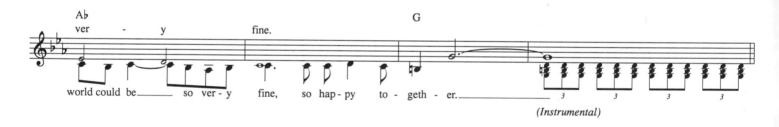

ver - y   fine.

world could be___ so ver-y fine,   so hap-py to-geth-er.___
(Instrumental)

I   can see me   lov-in' no-bod-y but   you   for all my life.___
(Ah)_____

When you're with me, ba-by, the skies___ will be   blue for all my life.
(Ah)_____

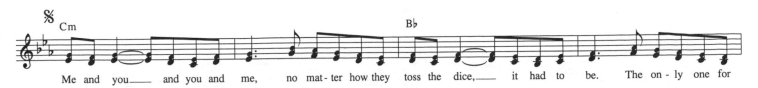

Me and you___ and you and me, no mat-ter how they toss the dice,___ it had to be. The on-ly one for

me is you,___ and you for me, so hap-py to-geth-er.___ (Instrumental)

(Instr.)

Ba ba ba ba ba ba ba ba ba ba ba.___

Ba ba ba ba ba ba ba ba ba ba ba.___

CODA

geth-er, ___ so hap-py to-geth-er, ___ and how is the weath-er? ___
(Ooh)___ (ooh)___ (Ba ba ba ba ba

___ So hap-py to-geth-er. ___ So hap-py to-geth-er. ___
ba ba ba ba ba ba ba ba ba ba ba ba ba ba ba ba.)___

HEARTBREAK HOTEL

Words and Music by MAE BOREN AXTON,
TOMMY DURDEN and ELVIS PRESLEY

HERE, THERE AND EVERYWHERE

Words and Music by JOHN LENNON
and PAUL McCARTNEY

HIT ME WITH YOUR BEST SHOT

Words and Music by
EDDIE SCHWARTZ

I JUST FALL IN LOVE AGAIN

Words and Music by LARRY HERBSTRITT, STEPHEN H. DORFF,
GLORIA SKLEROV and HARRY LLOYD

I SHOT THE SHERIFF

Words and Music by
BOB MARLEY

Moderately slow, with a beat

(1.,5.) I shot the sher - iff, but I did not shoot the dep - u - ty.
(2.) I shot the sher - iff, but I swear it was in self - de - fense.
(3.) I shot the sher - iff, but I swear it was in self - de - fense.
(4.) I shot the sher - iff, but I did not shoot the dep - u - ty.

I shot the sher - iff, but I did - n't shoot the dep - u - ty.
I shot the sher - iff, and they say it is a cap - i - tal of - fense.
I shot the sher - iff, but I swear it was in self - de - fense.
I shot the sher - iff, but I did - n't shoot the dep - u - ty.

All a - round in my home - town, they're try - ing to track me down. They
Sher - iff John Brown al - ways hat - ed me, for what, I don't know. And
Free - dom came my way one day, and I start - ed out of town.
Re - flex - es got the bet - ter of me, and what is to be must be.

say they want to bring me in guilt - y for the kill - ing of a dep - u -
ev - 'ry time that I plant a seed, he said, "Kill it be - fore it
All of a sud - den, I see sher - iff John Brown aim - ing to shoot me
Ev - 'ry - day the buck - et goes to the well, but one day the bot - tom will

ty, for the life of a dep - u - ty. But I say:
grows." He said, "Kill it be - fore it grows." But I say:
down. So I shot, I shot him down. But I say:
drop out. Yes, one day the bot - tom will drop out. But I say:

1,2,3   **4**   **D.S. al Coda**

CODA

Fmaj7   Em7   Am   **Repeat ad lib.**   N.C.

rit.

I Want to Hold Your Hand

Words and Music by JOHN LENNON
and PAUL McCARTNEY

I WILL

Words and Music by JOHN LENNON
and PAUL McCARTNEY

I WILL FOLLOW HIM
(I Will Follow You)

English Lyric by NORMAN GIMBEL and ARTHUR ALTMAN
Original Lyric by JACQUES PLANTE
Music by J.W. STOLE and DEL ROMA

Early '60s Rock

(I'VE HAD) THE TIME OF MY LIFE

from DIRTY DANCING

Words and Music by DONALD MARKOWITZ,
JOHN DeNICOLA and FRANKIE PREVITE

Moderately

Now I've had the time of my life.___ No, I never felt___ like this be-

fore. Yes, I swear it's the truth,___ and I owe it all to you.___ 'Cause___

I've had the time of my life,___ and I owe it all to you._____

I've been

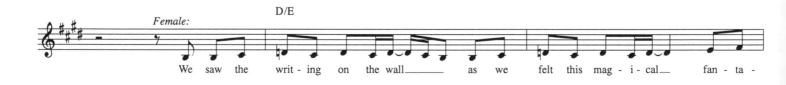

wait-ing for so long,___ now I've fi-n'lly found some-one___ to stand by me.___

We saw the writ-ing on the wall___ as we felt this mag-i-cal___ fan-ta-

sy.___ Now with pas-sion in our eyes,___ there's no way we could dis-guise___ it se-cret-

ly.___ So we take each oth-er's hand___ 'cause we seem to un-der-stand the ur-gen-

66

IF

Words and Music by
DAVID GATES

IMAGINE

Words and Music by
JOHN LENNON

You,_____ you may say_____ I'm a dream-er,

but I'm not the on-ly one.____ I hope some-day_____ you'll

join us_____ and the world_____ will be as one.____

I-mag-ine no_____ pos-ses- and the world_____ will live as one.____

IT'S MY PARTY

Words and Music by HERB WIENER,
WALLY GOLD and JOHN GLUCK, Jr.

No-bod-y knows_ where my John-ny has gone,_ but Ju-dy left_ the same time.
Play all my rec-ords, keep danc-ing all night,_ but leave me a-lone_ for a- while.
Ju-dy and John-ny just walked thru the door,_ like a queen_ with her king.

Why was he hold-ing her hand,_ when he's sup-posed_ to be mine?_____
'Til John-ny's danc-ing with me,_ I've got no rea-son to smile.____
Oh, what a birth-day sur-prise,_ Ju-dy's wear-ing his ring.____

It's my par-ty, and I'll cry if I want_ to, cry if I want_ to, cry if I want_ to.

You would cry, too, if it hap-pened to you.

IT'S STILL ROCK AND ROLL TO ME

Words and Music by
BILLY JOEL

IN MY LIFE

Words and Music by JOHN LENNON
and PAUL McCARTNEY

JUST ONE LOOK

Words and Music by DORIS PAYNE
and GREGORY CARROLL

JUST ONCE

Words by CYNTHIA WEIL
Music by BARRY MANN

JUST THE WAY YOU ARE

Words and Music by
BILLY JOEL

Let's Hang On

Words and Music by BOB CREWE,
SANDY LINZER and DENNY RANDELL

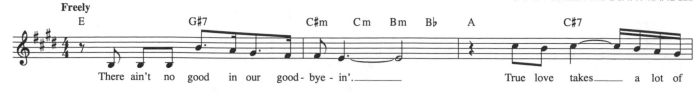

There ain't no good in our good-bye-in'._____ True love takes_____ a lot of

try-in'. Oh,_ I'm cry-in'. (Instr.)

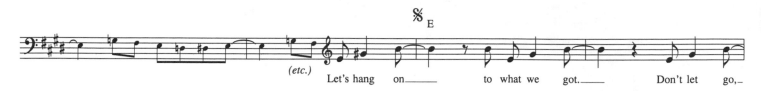

(etc.) Let's hang on_____ to what we got._____ Don't let go,_

_ girl, we got a lot. Got a lot of love be-tween us. Hang on,_

_ hang on,_ hang on_____ to what we got._____

You say you're gon-na go and call it quits,_ gon-na chuck it all_____ and break our

love to bits._____ I wish you nev-er said it. No, no, we'll

both re-gret it. That lit-tle chip of dia-mond on your hand_ ain't a for-tune, ba-by, but you

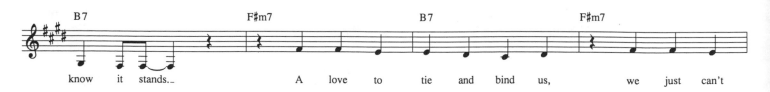

know it stands._____ A love to tie and bind us, we just can't

LET'S HANG ON - Background vocals

Let's hang on ___ to what we got. ___ Don't let go,

___ girl, we got a lot. Got a lot ___ of ___ love be - tween us. Hang on,

___ hang on, ___ hang on, ___ doot, ___ doot, ___ doot. ___

Break it up. _____ Break it up. _____

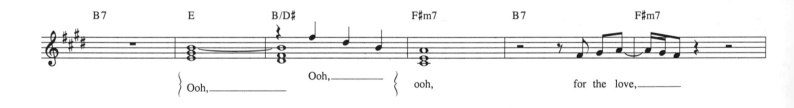

Ooh, _____ Ooh, _____ ooh, for the love, _____

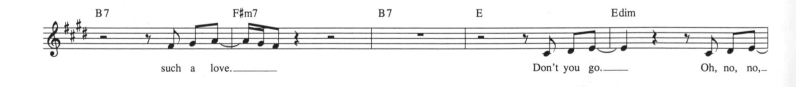

such a love. _____ Don't you go. _____ Oh, no, no, ___

___ think it o - ver and stay - ay. Let's hang on ___ to what we got. ___ Don't let go, ___

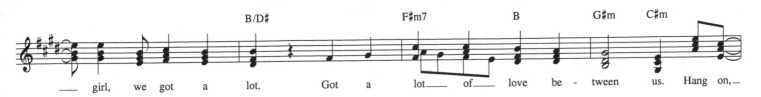

girl, we got a lot. Got a lot___ of___ love be - tween us. Hang on,___

___ hang on,___ hang on,___ doot,___ doot,___ doot. Ah, Ah,___

ah. ah.___

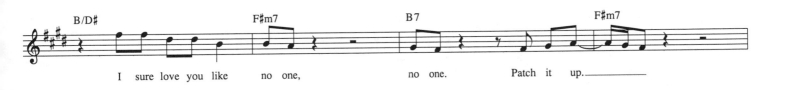

I sure love you like no one, no one. Patch it up.___

Patch it up.___ Cry - in', cry - in', cry - in', I'm

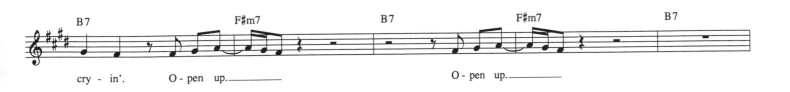

cry - in'. O - pen up.___ O - pen up.___

Don't you go.___ Oh, no, no,___ think it o - ver and stay - ay. Let's hang on___

LET'S HEAR IT FOR THE BOY
from the Paramount Motion Picture FOOTLOOSE

Words by DEAN PITCHFORD
Music by TOM SNOW

Moderately Bright

1. My

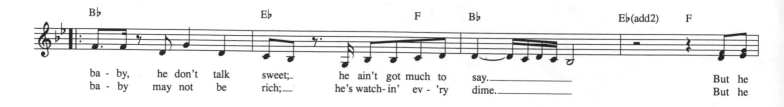

ba - by, he don't talk sweet; he ain't got much to say. But he
ba - by may not be rich; he's watch-in' ev - 'ry dime. But he

loves me, loves me, loves me. I know that he loves me an - y - way. And
loves me, loves me, loves me. We always have a real good time. And

may - be he don't dress fine, but I don't real - ly mind. 'Cause
may - be he sings off key, but that's all right by me, yeah. But

ev - 'ry time he pulls me near I just want to cheer. Let's
what he does he does so well. Makes me wan - na yell. Let's
ev - 'ry time he pulls me near I just want to cheer.

hear it for the boy.

Let's give the boy a hand. Let's

hear it for my ba - by, you know you got to un - der - stand.

Oh,_____ may - be he's_ no Ro - me - o,_____ but he's my lov- in' one__ man show.

To Coda ⊕

Oh, wo, wo, wo. Let's hear it for the boy._____

My

D.S. al Coda

'Cause

CODA ⊕

wo. Let's hear it for_ the boy._____

Let's hear it for the boy._____

Let's hear it for my man._

Let's hear it for my ba - by.

Repeat ad lib.

Let's hear it for_ the boy._____

LIDO SHUFFLE

Words and Music by BOZ SCAGGS
and DAVID PAICH

Rock Shuffle

Li - do missed___ the boat___ ___ that day___ he left___ the shack, ___ but that___

___ was all___ he missed, ___ and he ain't com - in' back.___ In a

tomb-stone bar in a juke-joint car___ he made___ a stop___ just long___
Li - do be run-nin' hav-in' great big fun un-til he got___ the note___ say-ing, "Tow

___ e - nough to grab___ the han - dle off___ the top.___ Next___
___ the line___ or blow it," and that___ was all___ she wrote. He be mak -

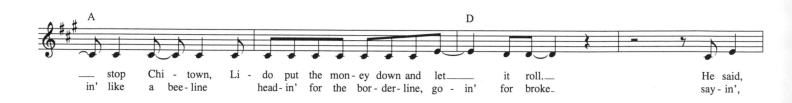

___ stop Chi - town, Li - do put the mon - ey down and let___ it roll.___ He said,
in' like a bee - line head-in' for the bor - der-line, go-in' for broke___ say - in',

"One more___ job___ ought to get it, one last___ shot___ 'fore we quit it,
"One more___ hit___ ought to do it, this joint___ ain't___ noth - in' to it,

one for the road." Li - do,
one more for the road."

oh, he's for the mon-ey, he's for the show,-

Li - do's a-wait-in' for the go. Li - do,— oh.

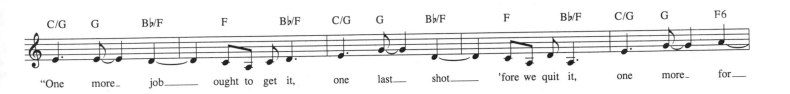

"One more job ought to get it, one last shot 'fore we quit it, one more for

the road." Li -

THE LOCO-MOTION

Words and Music by GERRY GOFFIN
and CAROLE KING

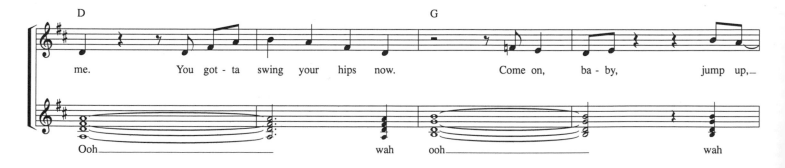

LOVE SNEAKIN' UP ON YOU

Words and Music by JIMMY SCOTT
and TOM SNOW

that's just love___ sneak-in' up on you. Hey, hey.___

up on you.___ Hey,_____ yeah.

D.S. al Coda

up on you.___ Well,_____ Don't wor - ry, ba - by. It ain't noth - ing new.___

That's just love___ sneak-in' up on you.___ If your whole world is shak - in'___ and you

feel like_ I do,___ that's just love___ sneak-in' up on you.___ Well, now, up on you.___

Me and Bobby McGee

Words and Music by KRIS KRISTOFFERSON
and FRED FOSTER

MAYBE BABY

By NORMAN PETTY
and CHARLES HARDIN

MISSING YOU

Words by JOHN WAITE
Music by JOHN WAITE,
CHAS SANDFORD and MARK LEONARD

MY BOYFRIEND'S BACK

Words and Music by ROBERT FELDMAN,
GERALD GOLDSTEIN and RICHARD GOTTEHRER

Moderately

Spoken: He went away, and you hung around and bothered me every night.

And when I wouldn't go out with you, you said things that weren't very nice.   My

(Hey la hey la, my boy-friend's back)

boy - friend's back, and you're gon - na be in trou - ble.
He's been gone for____ such a long____ time.____   When you

(Hey la hey la, my boy-friend's back)

see him com - in', bet - ter cut on the dou - ble.
Now he's back____ and____ things will be fine.____   You're

(Hey la hey la, my boy-friend's back)

You've been spread-in' lies that I was un - true.____
gon - na be____ sor - ry you were ev - er born____   So
'cause he's

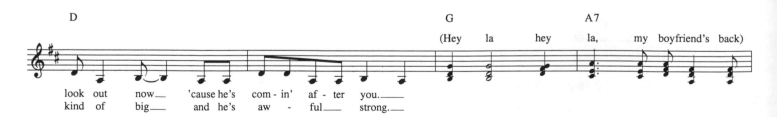

(Hey la hey la, my boyfriend's back)

look out now____ 'cause he's com - in' af - ter you.____
kind of big____ and he's aw - ful strong.____

Hey,_____ he knows that you've been try-in', and_____ he knows that you've been ly-in'.
Hey,_____ he knows I was-n't cheat-in', now_____ you're gon-na get a beat-in'.
Hey,_____ I can see him com-in', now_____ you bet-ter start a-run-nin'.

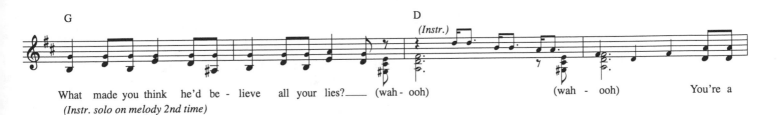

What made you think he'd be-lieve all your lies?____ (wah - ooh) (wah - ooh) You're a
(Instr. solo on melody 2nd time)

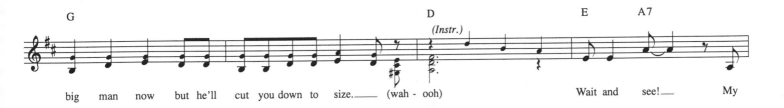

big man now but he'll cut you down to size.____ (wah - ooh) Wait and see!____ My

To Coda ⊕

(Hey la hey la, my boy-friend's back)

boy-friend's back, he's gon-na save my rep-u-ta-tion. If

D.S. al Coda

(Hey la hey la, my boy-friend's back)

I were you I'd take a per-ma-nent va-ca-tion.

CODA

Repeat ad lib. | **Last time**

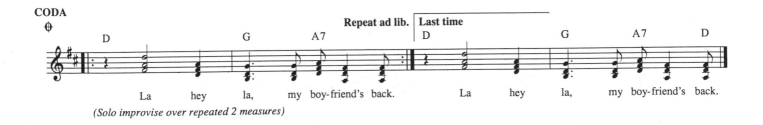

La hey la, my boy-friend's back. La hey la, my boy-friend's back.
(Solo improvise over repeated 2 measures)

(You Make Me Feel Like)
A NATURAL WOMAN

Words and Music by GERRY GOFFIN,
CAROLE KING and JERRY WEXLER

NEW YORK STATE OF MIND

Words and Music by
BILLY JOEL

Slowly, with a blues feel

(1.) Some folks_ like to get a-way, take a hol-i-day from the neigh-bor-hood,
(2.) I've seen_ all the mov-ie stars in their fan-cy cars and their lim-ou-sines,
(3.,5.) Comes down_ to re-al-i-ty, and it's fine with me 'cause I've let it slide.
(4.) *Instrumental*

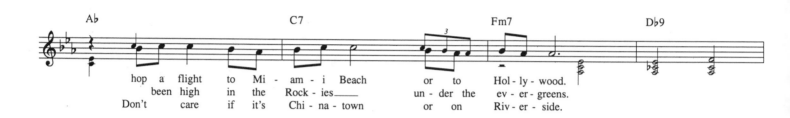

hop a flight to Mi-am-i Beach or to Hol-ly-wood.
been high in the Rock-ies or un-der the ev-er-greens.
Don't care if it's Chi-na-town or on Riv-er-side.

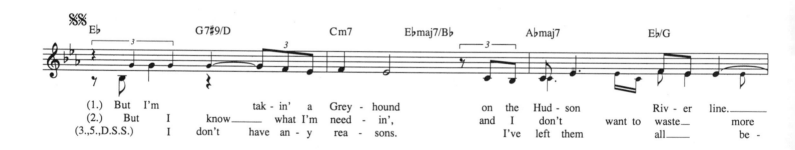

(1.) But I'm tak-in' a Grey-hound on the Hud-son Riv-er line.
(2.) But I know_____ what I'm need-in', and I don't want to waste_ more
(3.,5.,D.S.S.) I don't have an-y rea-sons. I've left them all_____ be-

time.
hind.

I'm in a New York_____ state of mind.

To Coda ⊕

1,3,5 | **D.S.S. al Coda after verse 5** | **2,4**

It was so eas - y____ liv - in' day by day,____

out of touch with the rhy - thm and blues.

And now I need a lit - tle give and take.____ The New York Times,____

D.S. for verses 3, 5

____ the Dai - ly News.____

CODA

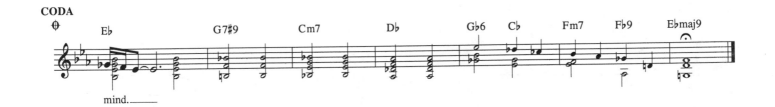

mind.____

THE NEXT TIME I FALL

Words and Music by PAUL GORDON
and BOBBY CALDWELL

ONE FINE DAY

Words and Music by GERRY GOFFIN
and CAROLE KING

D.S. al Coda

CODA

Repeat ad lib.

ONE LESS BELL TO ANSWER

Lyric by HAL DAVID
Music by BURT BACHARACH

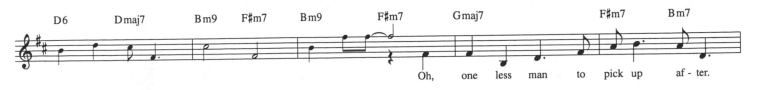

Oh, one less man to pick up af-ter.

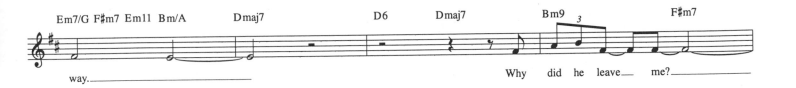

No more laugh-ter, no more love ____ since he went, oh, he went a-

way. ____ Why did he leave ____ me? ____

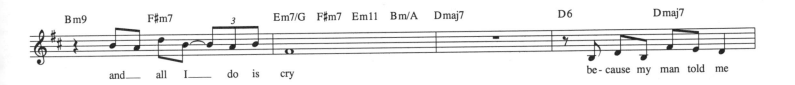

Now I've got one less egg to fry, one less egg to fry, ____

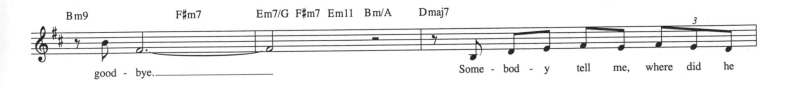

and ____ all I ____ do is cry be-cause my man told me

good - bye. ____ Some-bod-y tell me, where did he

go? Why did he go? Tell me, how could he leave me?

ONE LESS BELL TO ANSWER - Background vocals

ONLY THE LONELY
(Know the Way I Feel)

Words and Music by ROY ORBISON
and JOE MELSON

PIECE OF MY HEART

Words and Music by JERRY RAGOVOY
and BERT BERNS

SO FAR AWAY

Words and Music by
CAROLE KING

Save the Best for Last

Words and Music by PHIL GALDSTON,
JON LIND and WENDY WALDMAN

SAVING ALL MY LOVE FOR YOU

Words by GERRY GOFFIN
Music by MICHAEL MASSER

SOMETIMES WHEN WE TOUCH

Words by DAN HILL
Music by BARRY MANN

Slowly, in 2

You

ask me if___ I love___ you,___ and I choke on my re-ply.___ I'd
mance and all___ its strat-e-gy leaves me bat-tling with my pride.___ But
times I un-der-stand___ you,___ and I know how hard___ you've tried.___ I've

rath-er hurt___ you hon-est-ly___ than mis-lead you with___ a lie. And
through the in-se-cu-ri-ty___ some ten-der-ness___ sur-vives. I'm
watched while love com-mands___ you,___ and I've watched love pass___ you by. At

who am I___ to judge___ you on what you say or do? I'm
just an-oth-er writ-er still trapped with-in my truths; a
times I think___ we're drift-ers, still search-ing___ for a friend, a

on-ly just___ be-gin-ning to see the real___ you.
hes-i-tant prize-fight-er still trapped with-in___ my youth.
broth-er or___ a sis-ter. But then the pas-sion flares___ a-gain.

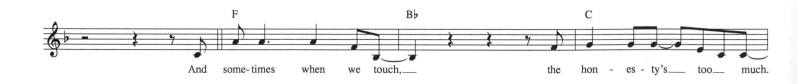

And some-times when we touch,___ the hon-es-ty's___ too___ much.

___ And I have to close___ my eyes___ and___ hide.___

I wan-na hold you till___ I die,___ till we both break down___ and cry.___

To Coda ⊕ | **1**

___ I wan-na hold you till the fear___ in me___ sub - sides.

2

Ro - sides. At

times I'd like___ to break___ you and drive___ you to___ your knees.___ At

D.S. al Coda

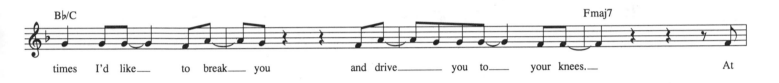

times I'd like___ to break___ through and hold_ you end - less-ly.___ At

CODA
⊕

sides.___

SOMEWHERE OUT THERE
from AN AMERICAN TAIL

Words and Music by JAMES HORNER,
BARRY MANN and CYNTHIA WEIL

Moderately, with expression

Female:
Some-where out there, be-neath the pale moon-light,

some - one's think-in' of me and lov-ing me to-night. *Male:* Some-where out____

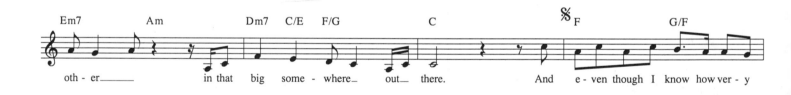

____ there,____ some - one's say - ing a prayer____ that we'll find one an -

oth - er____ in that big some - where____ out____ there. And e - ven though I know how ver - y

far a - part____ we are,____ it helps to think____ we might be wish - in' on the same____ bright - star. *Female:* And

when the night wind starts to sing a lone - some lull - a - by, it helps to think we're sleep-ing un - der-

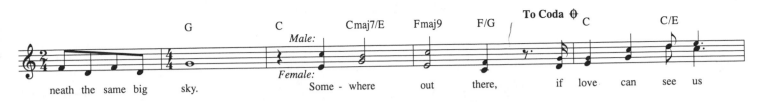

neath the same big sky.

Male:
Female:
Some - where out there, if love can see us

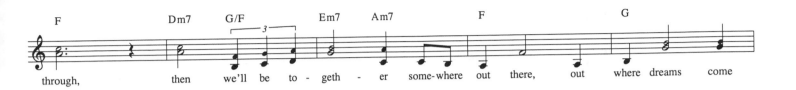

through, then we'll be to - geth - er some-where out there, out where dreams come

true.

And

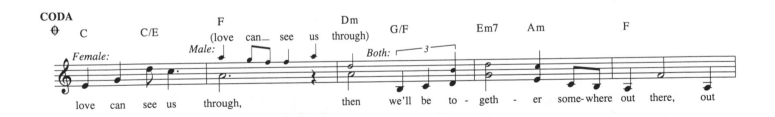

love can see us through, then we'll be to - geth - er some-where out there, out

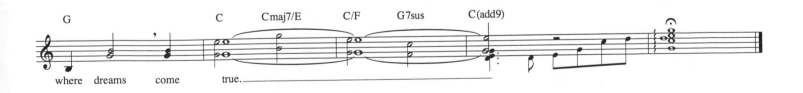

where dreams come true.

STAND BY ME

Words and Music by BEN E. KING,
JERRY LEIBER and MIKE STOLLER

SEA OF LOVE

Words and Music by GEORGE KHOURY
and PHILIP BAPTISTE

STEAMROLLER
(Steamroller Blues)

Words and Music by
JAMES TAYLOR

STRAIGHT UP

Words and Music by
ELLIOT WOLFF

SWEET DREAMS
(Are Made of This)

Words and Music by DAVID A. STEWART
and ANNIE LENNOX

Hold your head up. Keep your head up, mov-in' on.— Hold your head up, mov-in' on.—

Keep your head up, mov-in' on.— Hold your head up, mov-in' on.— Keep your head up, mov-in' on.—

Hold your head up, mov-in' on.— Keep your head up.

D.S. al Coda

CODA

Sweet dreams are made of this.— Who am— I— to dis-a-gree?— I

Repeat ad lib.

tra-vel the world— and the sev-en seas.— Ev-'ry-bod-y's look-ing for some-thing.

(vocals may continue over the ending)

Tears in Heaven

Words and Music by ERIC CLAPTON
and WILL JENNINGS

have you beg-gin' please,___ beg-gin' please.___

Be - yond the door___

there's peace, I'm sure.___ And I know___ there'll be no more___ tears in heav-

en.

CODA

en.

THAT'LL BE THE DAY

Words and Music by JERRY ALLISON,
NORMAN PETTY and BUDDY HOLLY

THAT'LL BE THE DAY - Background vocals

THIS MASQUERADE

Words and Music by
LEON RUSSELL

Turn the Beat Around

Words and Music by PETER JACKSON Jr.
and GERALD JACKSON

TWIST AND SHOUT

Words and Music by BERT RUSSELL
and PHIL MEDLEY

TIME AFTER TIME

Words and Music by CYNDI LAUPER
and ROB HYMAN

UNDER THE BOARDWALK

Words and Music by ARTIE RESNICK
and KENNY YOUNG

*Background "Ooh", 2nd verse.

UNCHAINED MELODY

Lyric by HY ZARET
Music by ALEX NORTH

Slow '50s Ballad

(Instr.) Oh, my love, my dar - ling, I've hun - gered for your

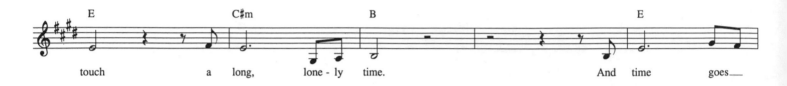

touch a long, lone - ly time. And time goes

by so slow - ly, and time can do so much. Are
(so much)

you still mine? I need your love. I
(Are you still mine?)

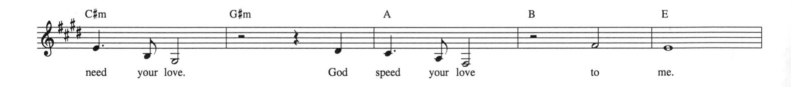

need your love. God speed your love to me.

(Instr.) Lone - ly riv - ers flow to the sea, to the sea,

to the o - pen arms of the sea. Lone - ly riv - ers sigh, "Wait for

me,_____ wait for me." I'll be_____ com-ing home,_____ wait for me. Oh, my_____

love, my dar-ling, I've hun-gered, hun-gered_____ for your touch a long, lone-ly

time And time goes_____ by so slow-ly, and

time can do so much. Are_____ you still mine?_____ I_____

need_____ your_____ love. I, I need your love. God speed your love

to me.

UP ON THE ROOF

Words and Music by GERRY GOFFIN
and CAROLE KING

UP WHERE WE BELONG
from the Paramount Picture AN OFFICER AND A GENTLEMAN

Words by WILL JENNINGS
Music by BUFFY SAINTE-MARIE and JACK NITZSCHE

WAY OVER YONDER

Words and Music by
CAROLE KING

Gospel Blues

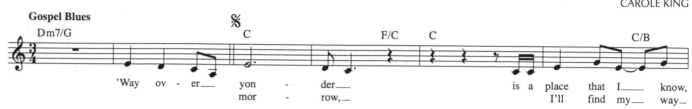

'Way ov-er yon - der____ is a place that I____ know,
mor - row,____ I'll find my____ way

____ where I can find____ shel - ter
to the land where the____ hon - ey runs

from____ hun - ger and____ cold.
in riv - ers each____ day. And the

sweet tast - in' good____ life____ is so eas - i - ly found.

'Way o - ver yon - der,____ that's where I'm____ bound.

I know____ when I get there,____ the

first thing I'll see____ is the sun____ shin-ing gold - en,

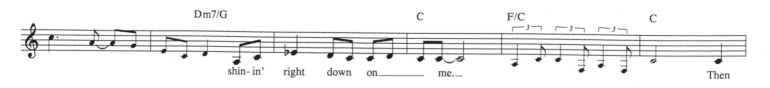

shin-in' right down on____ me.____ Then

149

trou - ble's gon - na lose_____ me,_____ wor - ry leave___ me be - hind,_____

_____ and I'll stand up proud - ly_____ in true peace of

mind. Talk - in' 'bout a, talk - in' 'bout a - way o - ver yon - der___

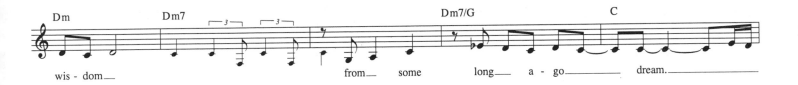

is a place I have seen.___ It's a gar - den of

wis - dom___ from___ some long a - go___ dream.___

May - be___ to -

WE GOT THE BEAT

Words and Music by
CHARLOTTE CAFFEY

CODA

yeah,   we got it!   (We got the beat.)

Ev-'ry-bod - y   get off your feet. (We got the beat.)   We know you can   dance to the beat. (We got the beat.)

Jump back,_____   get down.   'Round and 'round and 'round.
                     (We got the beat.)

(We got the beat.)   We got the beat. (We got the beat.)   We got the beat.

(We got the beat.)   (We got the beat.) We got the beat. (We got the beat.)   (We got the beat.) We got the beat!

WEDDING BELL BLUES

Words and Music by
LAURA NYRO

so,   I   al-ways   will.___   And though   de - vo - tion   rules   my   heart,   I   take   no
(Ooh)_____

bows.   Oh,   but   Bill,   you're   nev - er   gon - na   take___   those   wed - ding   vows..
___   (Take   no   bows)___

___   (Wed-ding   vows)___   Come   on,   Bill.___   (Come   on,   Bill.)___   So come   on,   Bill.___   (Come   on,   Bill.)_
(vows)_____   (Bill,_____   oh,   Bill)

___   Come   on   and   mar - ry   me,   Bill._____   I   got   the   wed - ding   bell   blues._____
(Bill)_____   (blues)___

Please,   mar - ry   me,   Bill._____   I   got   the   wed - ding   bell   blues.___
(Bill)_____   (blues)___

WE JUST DISAGREE

Words and Music by
JIM KRUEGER

WHERE THE BOYS ARE

Words and Music by HOWARD GREENFIELD
and NEIL SEDAKA

WHY

Words and Music by
ANNIE LENNOX

WILL YOU LOVE ME TOMORROW
(Will You Still Love Me Tomorrow)

Words and Music by GERRY GOFFIN
and CAROLE KING

WILD THING

Words and Music by
CHIP TAYLOR

WOOLY BULLY

Words and Music by
DOMINGO SAMUDIO

Moderately

(Instr.)

Mat-ty told Hat-ty_____ a-bout a thing she saw._____ Had
Hat-ty told Mat-ty,_____ "Let's don't take no chance.
Mat-ty told Hat-ty,_____ "That's the thing to do.___

two big horns____ and a wool-y jaw.__ } Wool-y Bul-ly,_____
Let's not be L sev-en. Come and learn to dance." }
Get yo' some-one real-ly to pull the wool with you."_ }

_____ Wool-y Bul-ly,___ Wool-y Bul-ly,___ Wool-y Bul-ly,___ Wool-y

To Coda ⊕ 1. E7 2. E7 A7

Bul-ly.

A7

(Sax solo)

D7 A7

E7 D7 A7 E7 D.S. al Coda

CODA ⊕ E7 A7

YESTERDAY

Words and Music by JOHN LENNON
and PAUL McCARTNEY

YOU'VE GOT A FRIEND

Words and Music by
CAROLE KING

YOUR SONG

Words and Music by ELTON JOHN
and BERNIE TAUPIN

THE ULTIMATE COLLECTION OF
FAKE BOOKS

The Ultimate Fake Book – 2nd Edition

Over 1200 songs, including: All I Ask of You • All the Things You Are • Always • And So It Goes • Autumn in New York • Blue Skies • Body and Soul • Call Me Irresponsible • Can't Help Falling in Love • Caravan • Easter Parade • Endless Love • Heart and Soul • The Impossible Dream • Isn't It Romantic? • The Lady Is a Tramp • Lay Down Sally • Let's Fall in Love • Moon River • My Funny Valentine • Piano Man • Roxanne • Satin Doll • Sophisticated Lady • Speak Low • Splish Splash • Strawberry Fields Forever • Tears in Heaven • A Time for Us (Love Theme from Romeo & Juliet) • Unforgettable • When I Fall in Love • When You Wish upon a Star • and hundreds more!

00240024 C Edition $45.00
00240025 E♭ Edition $45.00
00240026 B♭ Edition $45.00

Best Fake Book Ever – 2nd Edition

More than 1000 songs from all styles of music, including: All My Loving • American Pie • At the Hop • The Birth of the Blues • Cabaret • Can You Feel the Love Tonight • Don't Cry for Me Argentina • Dust in the Wind • Fever • Free Bird • From a Distance • The Girl from Ipanema • Hello, Dolly! • Hey Jude • I Heard It Through the Grapevine • The Keeper of the Stars • King of the Road • Longer • Misty • Route 66 • Sentimental Journey • Somebody • Somewhere in Time • Song Sung Blue • Spanish Eyes • Spinning Wheel • Take the "A" Train • Unchained Melody • We Will Rock You • What a Wonderful World • Wooly Bully • Y.M.C.A. • You're So Vain • and hundreds more.

00290239 C Edition $45.00
00240083 B♭ Edition $45.00
00240084 E♭ Edition $45.00

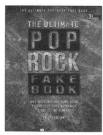

The Ultimate Pop/Rock Fake Book – 3rd Edition

Over 500 pop standards and contemporary hits, including: Addicted To Love • Ain't No Mountain High Enough • All Shook Up • Another One Bites The Dust • Can You Feel The Love Tonight • Crocodile Rock • Crying • Don't Know Much • Dust in the Wind • Earth Angel • Every Breath You Take • Have I Told You Lately • Hero • Hey Jude • Hold My Hand • Imagine • Layla • The Loco-Motion • Maggie May • Me and Bobby McGee • Mission: Impossible Theme • Oh, Pretty Woman • On Broadway • The Power of Love • Save the Best for Last • Spinning Wheel • Stand by Me • Stayin' Alive • Tears in Heaven • True Colors • The Twist • Vision Of Love • What's Going On • A Whole New World • Wild Thing • Wooly Bully • Yesterday • You've Lost That Lovin' Feelin' • and many more!

00240099 $35.00

The Ultimate Jazz Fake Book

Over 625 jazz classics spanning more than nine decades and representing all the styles of jazz. Includes: All of Me • All The Things You Are • Basin Street Blues • Birdland • Desafinado •Don't Get Around Much Anymore • A Foggy Day •I Concentrate On You •In The Mood • Take The "A" Train • Yardbird Suite • and many more!

00240079 C Edition $39.95
00240081 E♭ Edition $39.95
00240080 B♭ Edition $39.95

The Ultimate Broadway Fake Book - 4th Edition

More than 670 show-stoppers from over 200 shows! Includes: Ain't Misbehavin' • All I Ask Of You • As If We Never Said Goodbye • Bewitched • Camelot • Memory • Don't Cry For Me Argentina • Edelweiss • I Dreamed A Dream • If I Were A Rich Man • Oklahoma • People • Seasons Of Love • Send In The Clowns • Someone • What I Did For Love • and more.

00240046 $39.95

The Classical Fake Book

An unprecedented, amazingly comprehensive reference of over 650 classical themes and melodies for all classical music lovers. Includes everything from Renaissance music to Vivaldi and Mozart to Mendelssohn. Lyrics in the original language are included when appropriate. Also features a composer "timeline."

00240044 $24.95

The Beatles Fake Book

200 songs including: All My Loving • And I Love Her • Back In The USSR • Can't Buy Me Love • Day Tripper • Eight Days A Week • Eleanor Rigby • Help! • Here Comes The Sun • Hey Jude • Let It Be • Michelle • Penny Lane • Revolution • Yesterday • and many more.

00240069 $25.00

The Ultimate Country Fake Book

Over 700 super country hits, including: Achy Breaky Heart • Act Naturally • The Battle Hymn Of Love • Boot Scootin' Boogie • The Chair • Friends In Low Places • Grandpa (Tell Me 'Bout The Good Old Days) • Islands In The Stream • Jambalaya • Love Without End, Amen • No One Else On Earth • Okie From Muskogee • She Believes In Me • Stand By Me • What's Forever For • and more.

00240049 $35.00

Wedding & Love Fake Book

Over 400 classic and contemporary songs, including: All For Love • All I Ask Of You • Anniversary Song • Ave Maria • Can You Feel The Love Tonight • Endless Love • Forever And Ever, Amen • Forever In Love • I Wanna Be Loved • It Could Happen To You • Misty • Saving All My Love • So In Love • Through The Years • Vision Of Love • and more.

00240041 $24.95

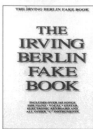

The Irving Berlin Fake Book

Over 150 Berlin songs, including: Alexander's Ragtime Band • Always • Blue Skies • Easter Parade • God Bless America • Happy Holiday • Heat Wave • I've Got My Love To Keep Me Warm • Puttin' On The Ritz • There's No Business Like Show Business • White Christmas • and many more.

00240043 $19.95

The Ultimate Christmas Fake Book - 3rd Edition

More than 200 holiday tunes, including: Blue Christmas • The Chipmunk Song • Frosty The Snowman • I Saw Mommy Kissing Santa Claus • I'll Be Home For Christmas • Jingle Bells • Rudolph, The Red-Nosed Reindeer • Silent Night • Silver Bells • and more!

00240045 $17.95

Gospel's Best – Words And Music

The best reference book of gospel music ever compiled! Here's a collection of over 500 of the greatest songs of our time, representing all areas of gospel music.

00240048 $24.95

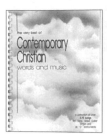

The Very Best Of Contemporary Christian Words & Music

More than 375 songs written and recorded by America's favorite Christian artists, including Amy Grant, Sandi Paul, Petra, Michael W. Smith, Bill & Gloria Gaither and many more.

00240067 $24.95

FOR MORE INFORMATION, SEE YOUR LOCAL MUSIC DEALER, OR WRITE TO:

HAL•LEONARD®
CORPORATION

7777 W. BLUEMOUND RD. P.O. BOX 13819 MILWAUKEE, WI 53213
http://www.halleonard.com
Prices, contents and availabilty subject to change without notice

0597

MUSICAL THEATRE COLLECTIONS
FROM HAL LEONARD

BROADWAY BELTER'S SONGBOOK

A great new collection for women singers. All the songs have been chosen especially for this type of voice, and the ranges and keys have been carefully selected. 30 songs, including: Broadway Baby • The Lady Is A Tramp • Everything's Coming Up Roses • I'd Give My Life To You (*Miss Saigon*) • Cabaret. 176 pages.

_____00311608 ....$16.95

THE SINGER'S MUSICAL THEATRE ANTHOLOGY

The most comprehensive collection of Broadway selections ever organized specifically for the singer. Each of the five volumes contains important songs chosen because of their appropriateness to that particular voice type. All selections are in their authentic form, excerpted from the original vocal scores. The songs in *The Singer's Musical Theatre Anthology*, written by such noted composers as Kurt Weill, Richard Rodgers, Stephen Sondheim, and Jerome Kern, are vocal masterpieces ideal for the auditioning, practicing or performing vocalist.

Soprano
46 songs, including: Where Or When • If I Loved You • Goodnight, My Someone • Smoke Gets In Your Eyes • Barbara Song • and many more.

_____00361071 ....$19.95

Mezzo-Soprano/Alto
40 songs, including: My Funny Valentine • I Love Paris • Don't Cry For Me Argentina • Losing My Mind • Send In The Clowns • and many more.

_____00361072 ....$19.95

Tenor
42 songs, including: Stranger In Paradise • On The Street Where You Live • Younger Than Springtime • Lonely House • Not While I'm Around • and more.

_____00361073 ....$19.95

Baritone/Bass
37 songs, including: If Ever I Would Leave You • September Song • The Impossible Dream • Ol' Man River • Some Enchanted Evening • and more.

_____00361074 ....$19.95

Duets
21 songs, including: Too Many Mornings • We Kiss In A Shadow • People Will Say We're In Love • Bess You Is My Woman • Make Believe • more.

_____00361075 ....$16.95

THE SINGER'S MUSICAL THEATRE ANTHOLOGY VOL. 2

More great theatre songs for singers in a continuation of this highly successful and important series, once again compiled and edited by Richard Walters. As is the case with the first volume, these collections are as valuable to the classical singer as they are to the popular and theatre performer.

Soprano, Volume 2
42 songs, including: All Through The Night • And This Is My Beloved • Vilia • If I Were A Bell • Think Of Me.

_____00747066 ....$19.95

Mezzo-Soprano/Alto, Volume 2
44 songs, including: If He Walked Into My Life • The Party's Over • Johnny One Note • Adalaide's Lament • I Hate Men • I Dreamed A Dream.

_____00747031 ....$19.95

Tenor, Volume 2
46 songs, including: Miracle Of Miracles • Sit Down, You're Rockin' The Boat • Giants In The Sky • Bring Him Home • Music Of The Night.

_____00747032 ....$19.95

Baritone/Bass, Volume 2
44 songs, including: Guido's Song from *Nine* • Bye, Bye Baby • I Won't Send Roses • The Surrey With The Fringe On Top • Once In Love With Amy.

_____00747033 ....$19.95

THE ACTOR'S SONGBOOK

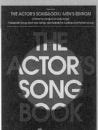

A wonderfully diverse collection of comedy songs, character songs, Vaudeville numbers, dramatic songs, and ballads for the actor who sings. A perfect resource to use for finding an audition song or specialty number. In two editions, one for women, and one for men, with a completely different selection of songs chosen for each edition. Over 50 songs in each book. Women's edition titles include: The Ladies Who Lunch • Cla-wence (Don't Tweat Me So Wough) • Cry Me A River • Shy • The Man That Got Away, and many more. Men's edition includes: Buddy's Blues (from *Follies*) • Doing The Reactionary • How to Handle A Woman • I'm Calm • Reviewing The Situation, many more.

_____00747035 Women's Edition $19.95
_____00747034 Men's Edition $19.95

FOR MORE INFORMATION, SEE YOUR LOCAL MUSIC DEALER, OR WRITE TO:

HAL•LEONARD®
CORPORATION
7777 W. BLUEMOUND RD. P.O. BOX 13819 MILWAUKEE, WI 53213

Prices, contents and availability subject to change without notice.

KIDS' BROADWAY SONGBOOK

An unprecedented collection of songs that were originally performed by children on the Broadway stage. A terrific and much needed publication for the thousands of children studying voice. Includes 16 songs for boys and girls: Gary, Indiana (*The Music Man*) • Castle On A Cloud (*Les Miserables*) • Where Is Love? (*Oliver!*) • Tomorrow (*Annie*) • and more.

_____00311609 ....$9.95

MUSICAL THEATRE CLASSICS

A fantastic series featuring the best songs from Broadway classics. Collections are organized by voice type and each book includes recorded piano accompaniments on CD – ideal for practicing. Compiled by Richard Walters, Sue Malmberg, pianist.

Soprano, Volume 1
13 songs, including: Climb Ev'ry Mountain • Falling In Love With Love • Hello, Young Lovers • Smoke Gets In Your Eyes • Wishing You Were Somehow Here Again.

_____00740036 ....$19.95

Soprano, Volume 2
13 more favorites, including: Can't Help Lovin' Dat Man • I Could Have Danced All Night • Show Me • Think Of Me • Till There Was You.

_____00740037 ....$19.95

Mezzo-Soprano/Alto, Volume 1
11 songs, including: Don't Cry For Me Argentina • I Dreamed A Dream • The Lady Is A Tramp • People • and more.

_____00740038 ....$19.95

Mezzo-Soprano/Alto, Volume 2
11 songs, including: Glad To Be Unhappy • Just You Wait • Memory • My Funny Valentine • On My Own • and more.

_____00740039 ....$19.95

Tenor
11 songs, including: All I Need Is A Girl • If You Could See Her • The Music Of The Night • On The Street Where You Live • Younger Than Springtime • and more.

_____00740040 ....$19.95

Baritone/Bass
11 classics, including: If Ever I Would Leave You • If I Loved You • Oh, What A Beautiful Mornin' • Ol' Man River • Try To Remember • and more.

_____00740041 ....$19.95

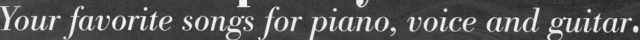